Beginner's guide to
Candlemaking
David Constable

SEARCH PRESS

First published in Great Britain 1997

Search Press Limited
Wellwood, North Farm Road,
Tunbridge Wells, Kent TN2 3DR

Reprinted 1998

ISBN 0 85532 832 0

The author would like to thank Sebastiano
Barbagallo of 15–17 Pembridge Road, London, for
supplying the dish that appears on the front cover;
and the Portishead Candle Company, Bristol, for
making the star-shaped sand candles on page 41.
    With special thanks to Graham Morgan and
Julie Speers, to Clint Twist and to Charlotte
de la Bedoyère and the Search Press team:
Roz Dace, John Dalton, Chantal Porter
and Julie Wood.

Suppliers
If you have difficulty in obtaining any of the
equipment or materials mentioned in this
book, then please write for further
information, either to the Publishers:

Search Press Ltd.,
Wellwood, North Farm Road,
Tunbridge Wells, Kent TN2 3DR

or to the author:

David Constable,
Candle Makers Suppliers,
28, Blythe Road, London W14

Printed in Spain by Elkar S. Coop, 48012 Bilbao

Contents

Introduction

Before gas and electricity, the naked flame as a light source was essential if life was to continue after sunset. Evidence of the use of candles has been found on prehistoric paintings on cave walls and in Egyptian tombs, and although there have been some changes, there is no essential difference between a candle made in the remotest past and one made today. Tallow and vegetable or insect waxes were the original fuels. Tallow candles gave off greasy smoke and an unpleasant smell, but they were reliable and cheap. The historian Pliny tells of candles in the first century AD being made of pitch with flax wicks, or molten wax into which a rush was dipped, and wax allowed to

harden. It is recorded that Romans used candles of both tallow and wax, especially beeswax. These simple materials were used until a wider range of suitable fuels became available in the nineteenth century. Stearin, originally produced from animal fat, was developed in the 1820's. Harder than tallow at room temperature, it produced no unpleasant odour and longer-lasting candles.

Recently, the discovery of petroleum oil and improved refining methods has made the production of large quantities of paraffin wax possible and today, paraffin wax, usually mixed with stearin, is predominantly used in candlemaking.

Today, we still employ the simple techniques used by our ancestors, but we are able to elaborate on these by using all the different colours, perfumes and tools that are now available to us. This book shows you how to make a variety of simple moulded, twisted, carved and decorated candles. Once you have mastered the basic techniques, you will be able to create beautiful candles to suit any mood or occasion

Equipment and materials

Equipment

Candlemaking equipment is neither expensive nor complicated. You probably already have most of the basic essentials at home, but any you do not have can be bought from craft shops or kitchen-ware suppliers.

Heat source

You need a heat source to melt the wax such as a gas or an electric cooker. Wax cools down quickly, so work near to your heat source.

Double boiler

This is used to heat the wax in and it should be made of stainless steel or aluminium. The capacity of the upper part should be at least 3l (5¼pt). If you do not have a double boiler, you can use one saucepan standing inside another, although uneven heating of the wax may result, so take extra care when checking temperatures.

A selection of basic equipment: washing-up bowl; dipping can; measuring jug; weighing scales; thermometers; wicking needles; double boiler.

Thermometer

Heated wax will remain liquid over a wide temperature range, but its inner structure changes as the temperature is increased. To make good candles you must work with the different types of wax at their ideal molten temperatures and you therefore need the right sort of thermometer. A candy or cooking thermometer is ideal – one that is calibrated between 38°C (100°F) and 180°C (356°F). These are available from craft shops and kitchen-ware suppliers.

Weighing scales

Ordinary kitchen scales can be used for weighing materials.

Measuring flask or jug

You need this to decide how much wax to melt for candle moulds. Fill the mould with water and then pour the water into a measuring jug. For every 10cc or 10g (10 fl oz) of water you will need 9g (9oz) of wax.

Dipping can

This is a tall cylindrical container used for holding liquid wax.

Bowl

Dipping cans have to be kept at the right temperature. A washing-up bowl filled with hot water can be used, whilst cold water can be used as a water bath to speed up the cooling process.

Iron

An iron can be used to smooth the base of a freshly made candle.

Hairdryer

The heat from a hairdryer can be used to soften the wax when making a candle, or to keep wax sheets pliable.

Pouring jug

A metal jug with an enclosed spout can be used to pour liquid wax into moulds.

Materials

The two essential ingredients for candles are wax and wicks. The wax burns and the wick transports liquid wax to the flame.

Wicking needle

This is a steel needle 100–250mm (4–10in) long. It is used to insert a wick into a mould and to secure the wick at the mould base.

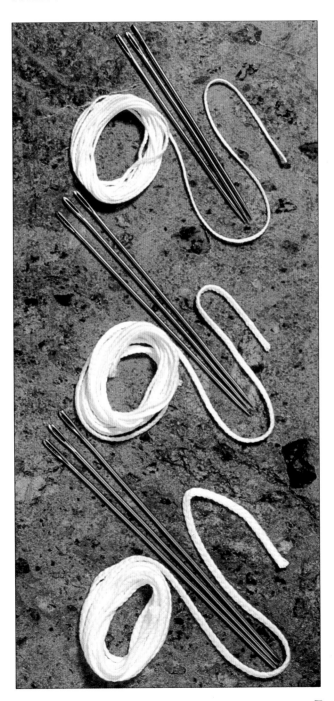

Wicking needles and wicks are available in a range of sizes.

Wick

Using the correct wick is very important. Candle wicks are made of specially braided cotton string – twine or cotton thread will not do! Most candles need a square braided wick which is produced in varying widths (see page 7) and graded according to the diameter of the finished candle: 12.5mm (½in), 25mm (1in), and so on. However, if a candle's length is less than 150mm (6in) a thinner wick can be used. If the candle is more than 150mm (6in), use the correct sized wick.

Do not allow an unprimed wick to become damp, or the candle will not burn.

Beeswax candles need a thicker, round braided wick of approximately twice the width needed for an ordinary candle.

A wire- or paper-cored wick is a stiffened wick which must be used with candles in containers.

Wax

There is a range of waxes available; some have a variety of applications, others have specific uses.

Paraffin wax This odourless, colourless wax is a by-product of the oil industry. It is the most suitable wax for candlemaking, and is inexpensive, clean and available in blocks, or in easy-to-use pellets.

Dip and carve wax This wax retains its malleability at lower temperatures. It is therefore a good wax to use for modelling.

Beeswax Used since ancient times for luxury candles, beeswax is more expensive and more difficult to work with than paraffin wax. The reward is the rich, redolent aroma of natural wax. It is available in bleached white or untreated shades of brown, is wholly natural and when melted, the liquid is opaque and viscous, almost like syrup. Added to paraffin wax, even in small quantities, it will increase the burning time of a candle. Modern church candles, for instance, are made with 25% beeswax. However, if more than 10% is used in a moulded candle, then a release agent must be applied to the mould beforehand.

Microcrystalline wax Also a by-product of the oil industry, this wax is opaque and yellow to off-white in colour. Various microcrystalline waxes are blended with paraffin wax to extend the hardness or softness of the wax.

Overdipping wax This gives a high-gloss final coat to an ordinary paraffin wax candle.

Chinese paraffin wax A cheap paraffin wax that is variable in quality and has a tendency to 'frost' internally and on the surface. Its peculiar translucent qualities can be exploited in candlemaking.

Additives

Additives enhance the performance and appearance of candles.

Stearin This is derived from palm oil and is used in most paraffin wax candles because it shrinks slightly on cooling, which helps release from moulds. It also improves the flame and burning time of a candle, and adds opacity and vibrancy to wax dyes – a useful ingredient indeed!

Plastic additive This is added to wax to improve its pliability.

Vybar Stearin cannot be used in rubber moulds because it chemically rots them. Vybar is used instead to improve the burning time and colour.

Wax glue

This is a soft, sticky type of wax which is used to glue two pieces of wax together, or to apply decorations and cut-outs to the surface of a candle.

Mould seal

A special reusable putty-like sealing compound used to secure the wick in the mould and to prevent the leakage of molten wax. It also prevents water from leaking into the mould while it is cooling in a water bath.

OPPOSITE

1. Dip and carve wax
2. Chinese paraffin wax
3. Beeswax sheet
4. White beeswax
5. Paraffin wax
6. Yellow beeswax
7. Vybar
8. Plastic additive
9. Wax glue
10. Hard microcrystalline wax
11. Soft microcrystalline wax

Dyes and perfumes

Soft, flattering candlelight is delightful and the glow of candles can enhance even an ordinary room, but colour and perfume can add a whole new dimension to candles in the home.

Creating colour

Although crayons and powder paint will colour wax, they are insoluble and will gather in the wick when the candle burns, causing spluttering and an unpleasant odour. Wax-soluble dye or candle pigment can be used for colouring wax for candlemaking.

Wax-soluble dye is available in disc form. Each disc will colour 2kg (4lb) of wax for casting in moulds, or 500g (1lb) for overdipping. The amount of dye required to give a particular shade will vary according to the blend and opacity of the wax mixture, and the bulk of the finished candle. To test for the finished colour, allow a teaspoon of the dyed wax to cool on a piece of greaseproof paper. The final colour will be apparent when the wax is completely cold.

A finely ground candle pigment can be used to colour wax for painting or surface decoration. It cannot be used to colour an entire candle as it clogs up the wick.

Although it is possible to mix dyes to the required shade, be careful not to over-dye the wax, as this will diminish the glow of the candle.

The amount of stearin used in a candle has a considerable effect on the opacity and brightness of wax dye. Whitening and pearlising agents can also be added to alter the colour of a candle.

Using perfumes

As well as enhancing a room with flickering light, candles can also please the olfactory senses. A huge choice of fragrances is available which means you can experiment at will, and never create unpleasant odours!

Care is needed when choosing your perfume. Candle perfumes are oil-soluble and they are specially formulated to be burned. The best of these use natural fruit and flower essences. If you want to use another type of perfume, always check that it is going to smell pleasant when burned. To do this, place a drop on the end of a piece of wick, ignite it, then blow it out. This will indicate what the perfume will smell like when it is added to a candle.

By varying the amounts of stearin, colours can be altered considerably. The opacity and brightness of the candles are also affected.

No stearin   *10% stearin*   *20% stearin*

A selection of beeswax sheets, pre-dyed wax beads, dye discs and candle perfume.

11

Common sense with wax

Most candlemaking techniques, and virtually all the candles described in this book, involve the use of molten, liquid wax. It is therefore essential that you are aware of the potential problems and know how to deal with them should they arise.

Working with heat

There are two ways of melting wax – a safe way and a less safe way.

The safe way is to use a double boiler, and for most candles this is perfectly adequate. The disadvantage is that a double boiler will not heat wax above 100°C (212°F), the boiling point of water.

Some candle waxes must be heated above this temperature and, in these cases, the wax must be heated in an open pan, which is a less safe method of melting wax. If you are using this method, it is very important that you do not leave the wax unattended. Raise the temperature slowly, monitoring it continuously with a thermometer to ensure that it does not overheat.

Fire safety

Wax should be treated like cooking oil. At temperatures below 100°C (212°F) it is fairly safe and will not ignite. At higher temperatures, it starts to vaporize and is liable to ignite. The exact temperature depends on the type of wax being used, but it is best to treat all waxes at temperatures above 100°C (212°F) as though they are highly flammable. If the wax does catch fire:

- Switch off the heat immediately and cover the flames with a damp cloth or a metal lid.
- Do not move the pan.
- Do not try to put out the fire with water.

Working with wax

Candlemaking is not an inherently messy occupation, but upsets are bound to occur. With a little thought, difficult situations can be dealt with easily, or avoided altogether.

Preventing accidents

- When making candles, wear old comfortable clothing and move or cover rugs and carpets.
- Give yourself enough space to work in and have your equipment and materials within easy reach.
- Remember that prolonged contact with hot molten wax will cause scalding. Do not leave pan handles sticking out from the heat source and keep children and pets away from hot wax containers.
- Do not pour liquid wax down a sink or drain – as it cools it sets hard and could cause a blockage.

Cleaning up

Allow spilt wax to cool and harden before trying to remove it.

- For wax on clothing and carpets, scrape off as much as possible and then remove the residue by ironing through a sheet of absorbent paper (kitchen towelling is ideal). Alternatively, you can have the item dry-cleaned.
- For wax on wood, scrape off the excess, then polish the residue with a soft cloth.
- For wax on metal or plastic, immerse the item in hot water until the wax melts and floats to the surface.
- White spirit or turpentine can be used to dissolve small amounts of cold wax.

Rigid and flexible moulds are used to shape wax into elegant and decorative candles.

Moulded candles

Moulds are available in a wonderful variety of shapes and sizes. You can use old containers – such as yoghurt pots, cardboard and plastic tubes – or choose from a bewildering range of inexpensive commercial moulds, from simple geometric forms to intricate ornate shapes. Despite the enormous variety of moulds, the basic technique is the same. A prepared wick is threaded through it, then molten wax is poured in. The mould is then cooled, and periodically topped up with wax. When the wax is cold, the candle is removed and the wick is trimmed. It sounds simple – and it is – but do read the following pages carefully and practise the technique. A little patience now might well save you time at a later date.

Rigid moulds

Rigid moulds are made of plastic, glass or metal. To increase the amount of shrinkage, a quantity (usually 10%) of stearin can be added to paraffin wax. A release agent must always be applied to the inside of the mould if you use more than 10% beeswax, because it is so sticky.

Plastic moulds are inexpensive and strong, and they are ideal for the beginner. Glass moulds have a good cooling rate. If you use these you will create superb high-gloss finish candles. However, they are fragile and limited to cylindrical shapes. Metal moulds are sturdy and cool very rapidly.

Flexible moulds

Flexible PVC and rubber moulds are used to make the more ornate candles, such as fruit and flowers, or those with intricate surface designs. They require constant attention during the cooling process, as they can distort, but it is worth spending extra time monitoring the process if you want a beautiful professional finish.

PVC moulds are ideal if you want candles with irregular shapes or embossed surfaces. These moulds can simply be rolled off the set candle without damaging the surface. Rubber moulds produce candles with a matt finish. They tend to deteriorate with repeated use, but are ideal for producing irregular shapes and high-relief surfaces.

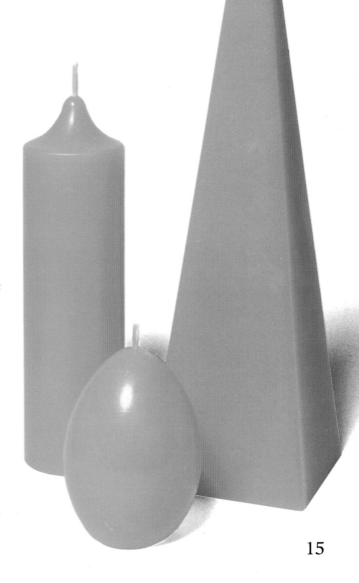

Rigid moulds

Rigid mould candles, using the most easily available type of commercial plastic moulds, are simple to make and are ideal for the beginner. All the basic moulding techniques are employed, and once you have created your first candle, you can move on to more sophisticated varieties. Always check the manufacturers' instructions thoroughly when using waxes and moulds.

Simple column candle

You will need

Cylindrical mould 100mm (4in) tall and 60mm (2¼in) in diameter
200g (7oz) paraffin wax
20g (²⁄₃oz) stearin
Wax dye
40mm (1½in) wick
Mould seal
Double boiler
Thermometer
Wicking needle
Pouring jug
Craft knife or scissors
Iron or saucepan

1. Add the stearin to the double boiler and melt it over a low heat.

2. When the stearin has melted, add one eighth of a dye disc and wait until it has dissolved.

3. Carefully add the paraffin wax. Heat it gently until it reaches 71°C (160°F), then switch off the heat.

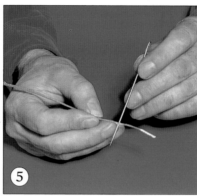

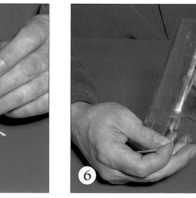

4. Cut a wick 50mm (2in) longer than the mould. Dip it into the molten wax for one minute to prime it. Straighten it between your fingers then hang it up for at least one minute.

5. The coated end of the primed wick should always be at the burning end of the candle. Push the wicking needle through the other end of the wick.

6. Thread the coated end of the primed wick through the small hole at the top of the mould.

7. Place the wicking needle across the base of the mould. Pull the wick tightly back through the top, and secure it with a lump of mould seal. Check that the seal is watertight by holding it under water.

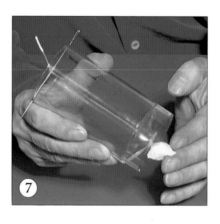

Wicking up

A good wick is at the heart of every good candle. The finished candle will not burn well if the wick is not primed correctly. Make sure it is central and straight when preparing a mould.

8. Heat the wax to 93°C (200°F). Transfer it to a pouring jug; check the temperature to ensure the wax is retaining its heat. Carefully pour the wax into the centre of the inverted mould and fill up to about 12mm (½in) from the top. Allow the wax to cool for two minutes, then give the mould a sharp tap with a spoon handle to dislodge any air bubbles. Leave to cool either at room temperature, or in a water bath (see page 19).

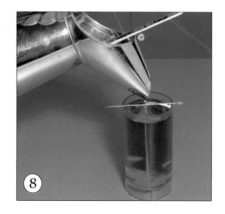

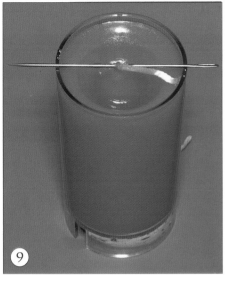

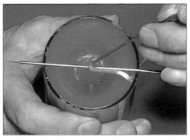

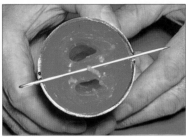

9. The wax starts to set from the bottom upwards and as it cools, a conical well forms round the wick. Below the skin the wax continues to cool and to shrink, forming a cavity below the surface. Break the skin with a wicking needle to gain access to the cavity beneath the surface. If the wax is still liquid inside, replace the mould in the water bath.

10. Reheat the wax to 93°C (200°F). Top up the cavity with hot wax. Do not fill the well beyond the original level, or the candle will be difficult to extract. Wiggle the wick to allow trapped air to escape, and pour in more wax if needed. Allow to cool at room temperature.

Filling the cavity

This photograph shows what will happen to the inside of a candle if the skin is not broken and if the cavity is not filled with liquid wax.

Water baths

Wax poured into a mould takes a long time to cool. Candles can be allowed to cool at room temperature, but you can speed up the cooling time by standing the mould in a large bowl of cold water. Water cooling improves the appearance of a candle and gives a smoother mould release.

Use a bowl with a level base and make sure that it is deep enough for the mould to stand upright in. The water should be level with the top of the wax. An ideal temperature is 10–15°C (50–60°F). If the water is below 10°C (50°F), thermal shock may cause cracking. Use a weight to keep the mould stable. Allow to cool for one hour.

11. To remove the mould, carefully peel away the mould seal. Turn the mould the right way up, and the candle will slide out easily.

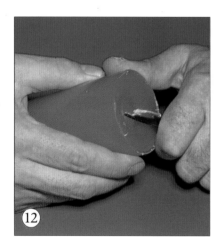

12. Remove the wicking needle. Carefully trim the wick flush to the base with a knife or a pair of scissors.

13. Flatten the base of the candle on the sole plate of a warm iron held over the wax saucepan. Alternatively, use a warm, empty saucepan. Trim the wick again if necessary.

The finished candle

Layered candles

You can alter the appearance of a column candle by pouring different coloured waxes into a mould in layers. Subtle toning shades, or bright eye-catching primary colours can add sparkle to festive occasions.

Follow steps 1–7 on pages 17 and 18, then fill the mould with layers of different colours. Each layer should be allowed to cool so that its surface becomes rubbery, before adding the next layer. Standing the mould at different angles produces wonderful effects. With practice, you will be able to create beautiful candles using this technique.

Pour the first layer into a mould. After one minute, tap the mould to release any air bubbles. Allow the wax to cool until the surface feels soft and rubbery – test by pressing it with a thermometer, or similar tool. Add another layer.

To make an angled layered candle, like the one below at the back of the picture, use the same technique but support the mould firmly at an angle as shown. Add multi-coloured layers as described left.

Keeping colours clean

When using different coloured waxes, clean out the double boiler and the pouring jug with tissue paper between each layer.

Candles can be layered using different shades of one colour, or a mixture of strong or complementary colours.

21

Flexible moulds

Beautifully ornate and intricate candles can be made using flexible moulds – candles with embossed surfaces decorated with twisted vines, animals, birds and flowers can be easily produced using the techniques shown. Unlike the rigid moulds, flexible moulds can simply be rolled off the set candle without damaging the surface. Always use unprimed wick with flexible moulds so as to limit the size of the hole made in the mould.

Single-colour candle

Here I use a mould stand to support the tulip mould, but you could use a jar or jug.

You will need

Flexible mould, 45mm
    (1³⁄₄in) in diameter,
    64mm (2¹⁄₂in) tall
80g (3oz) paraffin wax
1¹⁄₂tsp vybar
Wax dye
Wax perfume
25mm (1in) wick
Mould stand and
    cardboard
Double boiler
Thermometer
Wicking needle
Pouring jug
Craft knife or scissors
Iron or saucepan

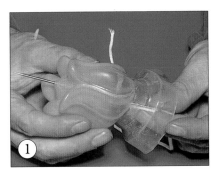

1. New moulds do not have a top opening for the wick. Pierce a small hole with a wicking needle and thread an unprimed wick up through the mould.

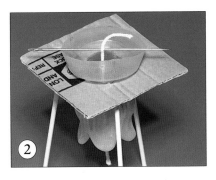

2. Make a cardboard template to support the mould on the stand. Use a wicking needle to support the wick in the centre of the mould.

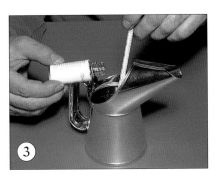

3. Heat the wax in a double boiler to 93°C (200°F). Add the vybar, and then an eighth of a dye disc (see page 17). Transfer the molten wax mixture into a warmed pouring jug, add a few drops of perfume and stir well.

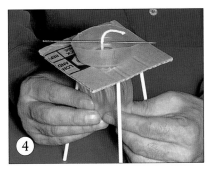

4. Pour the wax into the mould until it reaches the neck. Gently squeeze the mould to release any trapped air. As the wax cools, fill any cavities with molten wax (see page 19).

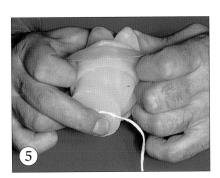

5. When the candle has set, smear the outside of the mould with liquid soap and carefully peel it back all the way round.

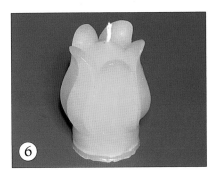

6. Trim the excess wick at the base, then flatten it with a warm iron (see page 20).

Pour-in pour-out candles

Layers of wax can be built up on the inside of a flexible mould by pouring the wax in and pouring it out. Beautiful, translucent effects can be created with just two layers. The colour will show through the outer layer if you colour the under layer (the second pour) with strong dye. Increasing the amount of dye will give you stunning results. Rigid or flexible moulds can be used, although flexible moulds create more interesting effects as the over layer varies in thickness, creating variable tones. This technique is ideal for capturing the translucency of flowers.

This project uses the same materials and equipment listed on page 23. Follow steps 1–6 on page 23, but make the following changes:

In step 3, heat the wax to 82°C (180°F). Add the vybar but do not add the dye disc.

In step 4, fill the mould with white wax, squeeze the mould to release trapped air, leave for five minutes until a hard layer forms and then pour the wax back into a pouring jug. Return all the wax to the double boiler, add a maximum of half a dye disc, reheat to 82°C (180°F) and then pour the coloured wax into the mould. As the wax cools, fill the cavities with molten wax (see page 19).

The finished candle

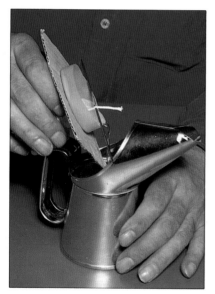

Fill a wicked mould with white wax. Allow it to cool for five minutes until a hard layer forms and then pour the molten wax back into a jug.

Colour the wax with dye and use it to fill the mould. Allow to cool. As the well forms, pierce it and top up the mould with molten wax.

The warm wax colours are enhanced by the flickering light of these candles as they burn, and the flowers glow as the deeper shades shine through.

Candles in containers

A variety of household containers can be adapted and used as decorative candleholders, including metal tins, bottles and jars. Before using them, check that they are watertight and, if they are not, block any gaps or holes with mould seal to prevent seepage.

The container is essentially the mould for this type of candle, but unlike a regular mould, the wick has to be suspended into the container using a wick sustainer.

As the candles burn, the molten wax is literally 'contained', so a special type of wick is required to burn off the excess wax. Choose a wire- or paper-cored wick and one with a diameter that corresponds to the size of the container. If a black deposit forms on the inside of the container, the wick is too large – extinguish the candle and do not relight it.

Using a wick sustainer

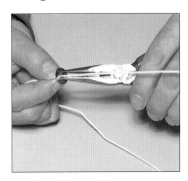

1. Thread a wick sustainer on to a primed wick, and tighten it with pliers.

2. Pour molten wax into the container until it is two thirds full. Thread a wicking needle through the other end of the wick. Drop the sustainer into the container and balance the needle on the rim.

Safety warning

It is important to take care when choosing and preparing these containers. The candles become oil lamps when the wax melts and inside a container, wax can become heated above its flash point and ignite. Also, if you choose to use a jam jar, badly annealed glass can shatter when heated. Make sure that any container candles are not left unattended when burning, and always place them on a flat surface.

Dipped candles

Dipping is the traditional way to make candles. Dipped candles have a beautiful tapered shape and can be made in a solid colour, or translucent effects can be created by adding a coating of dyed wax to a basic white candle. The technique is simple – repeating the wick priming process over and over again. By repeatedly dipping the wick in molten wax, you can build up any thickness of candle. The candles are dipped in a dipping can standing in a large pan of hot water – or you can use any tall metal or heatproof glass container. Candles are usually dipped in pairs and separated when they are cool.

Basic dipped candles

The materials listed for this project are sufficient to make six candles, 250mm (10in) tall and 12–20mm (½–¾in) in diameter.

You will need

3kg (6lb 10oz) paraffin wax

Wax dye for overdipping

Three 750mm (30in) lengths of 12mm (½in) wick

Metal dipping can 300mm (12in) tall

Large saucepan

Thermometer

Craft knife

1. Stand the dipping can in a saucepan half full of water; heat the water until the wax reaches a temperature of 71°C (160°F). Turn the heat down and soak a pair of wicks in the wax for one minute. Hang them up to dry.

2. When the wicks are cool, dip them back into the wax for about three seconds then allow them to cool for one to four minutes, depending on the room temperature.

3. Repeat the process until the candle is thick enough. If a wrinkled surface develops, the wax beneath the outer skin is still 'liquid' and is moving during dipping – wait longer between dips to rectify this.

Overdipped candles

Dramatic effects can be achieved with this simple technique. Once you have dipped your candles (see page 29), add a further 600g (1lb 5oz) of paraffin wax to the dipping can, heat it to 82°C (180°F) and add two dye discs.

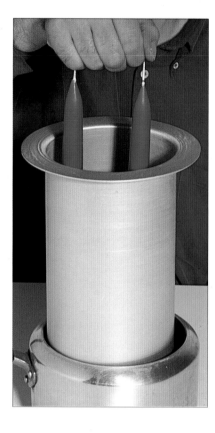

Dip the candles into the wax three times, leaving thirty seconds between each dip. Hang them up to cool.

Opposite
Loosely twisted and semi-twisted spiral candles are shown here. The double-wicked candles were twisted together while they were still warm.

Spiral candles

While dipped candles are still warm, they are malleable enough to model into other shapes. A spiral candle is simply a dipped candle flattened and then twisted.

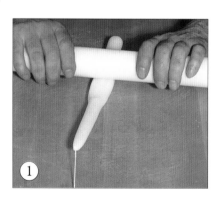

1. Use a dampened rolling pin on a damp surface to roll a warm dipped candle flat, working it down to about 6mm (¼in) thick. Do not roll the lower section, as this will be placed into a candle holder.

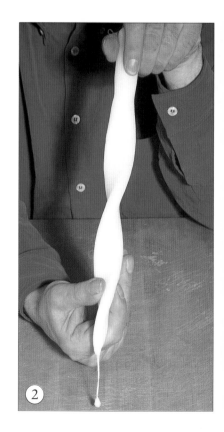

2. Twist the candle into a spiral by turning your hand as you draw your fingers up the taper. Keep twisting it until you are satisfied with the spiral. Trim the base flat and allow the candle to cool for one hour.

Using templates

As an alternative to traditional dipped candles, you can make your own wax sheets by dipping flat templates into liquid wax.

Properly cut and smoothed 6mm (¼in) thick glass makes an excellent template, but good quality plywood of the same thickness can be used. Allow room for holding the template during dipping; attach a string loop at the top to hang it up with during the cooling process.

If you are using a wooden template, first soak it in water, then wipe off any excess.

The quantities given for this project are sufficient to make a large quantity of candles. This amount of wax is required so as to fill the dipping cans. Any wax that you do not use, may be reheated and used again at a later date.

Begin by dividing the wax in half and transferring each half into separate dipping cans. Add chalky white dye to one of the cans, and a coloured dye to the other. Heat the wax (see step 1, page 29).

You will need

12kg (25lb) dip and carve wax

Wax dyes

12mm (½in) wick

Dipping cans

Large saucepans

Thermometer

Craft knife

Hairdryer

Iron

Making a spiral candle

1. Dip the template in white wax for two seconds. Hang it up to cool. Repeat the process to build up three layers, then overdip it three times in coloured wax. When the final layer has cooled, cut around the template with a craft knife.

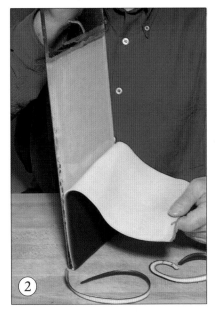

2. Peel the sheets from both sides of the template. Take care not to damage the wax surfaces.

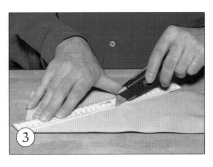

3. Cut one of the sheets into two triangles, and warm the wax surface with a hairdryer.

4. Cut a wick 20mm (³⁄₄in) longer than the side of the triangle. Lay it along the edge of the wax and fold the wax over the wick.

5. Roll the wax triangle into a fairly tight conical tube.

6. Flair out the exposed white edge with your fingers and smooth it into a spiral fin. Finish the candle by flattening the base with a warmed iron.

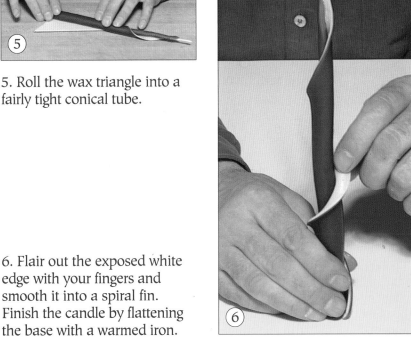

Floating candles

Dip and carve wax can be made into beautiful floating candles. Add a little perfume to create a stunning scented centrepiece for a special occasion. First melt the wax and prime the wicks (see pages 17 and 18).

You will need

200g (7oz) dip and carve wax
Wax dye
Rose-scented wax perfume
12mm (½in) wick, 50mm (2in) long
Double boiler
Thermometer
Greaseproof paper
Wax glue
Knife

1. Add twelve drops of perfume to the melted wax. Pour the wax on to a sheet of greaseproof paper.

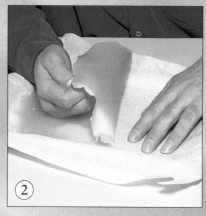

2. Allow the wax to cool until it is rubbery. Peel away the paper. If the wax is too hard, warm the surface with a hairdryer.

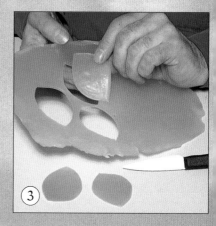

3. Carefully cut out petals of various sizes and curve them slightly with your fingers.

Fill a bowl with floating candles and create a glowing pool of light to adorn your table.

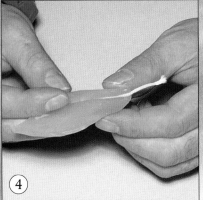

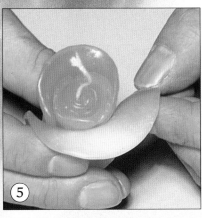

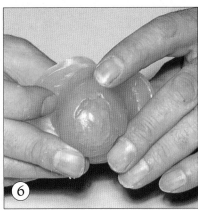

4. Squeeze two small petals around the wick and start to build up the flower.

5. Using wax glue, continue to build up the flower, gluing larger petals on until the rose is complete.

6. Finally, mould the candle base into a smooth round shape.

Beeswax sheets

These candles are made from preformed honeycomb sheets, which are beautifully textured. They are simple to make, and add elegance and a touch of class to any dinner table.

Beeswax sheets are approximately 300 x 200mm (12 x 8in) in size. They are workable at room temperature, although in cold weather they may need to be held near a heater for a few minutes until they soften, or you could use a hairdryer. Natural sheets are available in creamy white to rich medium brown; and dyed sheets can also be bought in a variety of colours.

<table>
<tr><td>You will need
Beeswax sheet
Round braided wick
Kitchen knife</td></tr>
</table>

Column candles

Beeswax sheet candles are simple to make. A sheet of wax will make a candle 300mm (12in) high and 20mm (^{3}/$_4$in) in diameter. This wax is best worked at a warm room temperature and candles should be rolled on a damp surface. You will need a beeswax wick, which is round, not flat like those used with paraffin wax candles.

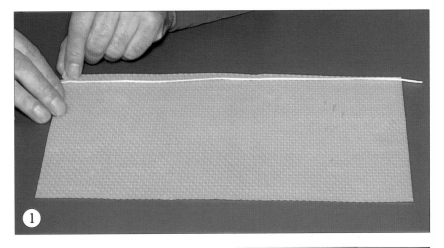

1. Cut a wick about 15mm (^{5}/$_8$in) longer than the length of the sheet. Lay it along one of the long edges of the sheet of wax, with one end protruding. Pinch a fingernail of wax from the bottom corner.

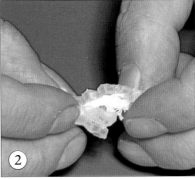

2. Squeeze the wax around and into the top of the wick.

3. Working on one area at a time, carefully turn the edge of the sheet over the wick.

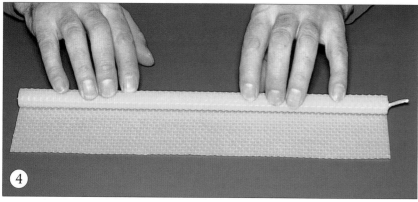

4. Roll the sheet smoothly keeping the ends square.

Spiral candles

You can make a spectacular spiral candle by simply using a triangle instead of a rectangle of beeswax.

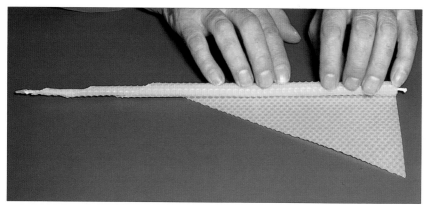

Cut a sheet of beeswax into a triangle, and roll it around the wick as shown above.

Multi-coloured spiral candles

To make a more unusual spiral candle, use two triangles of contrasting coloured wax. Trim 10mm (3/8in) off the base of one triangle, place the large triangle on top of the small one, aligning them at the base end. Add a wick and roll up as shown right.

Beeswax candles have a longer burning time than paraffin candles – and a wonderful aroma. This collection of column and spiral candles would grace any table.

Decorative candles

Beautiful decorated candles can be made easily, using just a few simple techniques. The surface of a candle can be embellished by painting, stencilling, carving, or by inserting corrugated card into the mould. You can also cast candles in sand. The candle must be set and cool before applying any decoration. Always follow the manufacturers' instructions when using any of the products for decoration. When using the spray paints, work in a well-ventilated area, and never use them near a naked flame.

Sand candles

Beautiful candles can be created from shapeless sand and wax – this is simple candlemaking at its very best. For sheer flickering, glowing effects, nothing compares with a sand candle, as the light soaks through the textured outer layer.

You will need

Bucket
Damp sand
475g (17oz) paraffin wax
Wax dye
7½tsp vybar or
   47.5g (1½oz) stearin
75 x 75mm (3 x 3in)
   timber
75mm (3in) length of
   medium container wick
Double boiler
Thermometer
Wicking needle
Pouring jug
Coarse file
Dividers
Metal modelling tool
Hairdryer

1. Part fill a bucket with damp sand. Place a block of wood, which will act as a former, on the sand, then pack more sand around its sides.

2. Level the sand then remove the wood to leave a sand mould. Melt the wax, heating it to 127°C (261°F), then dye it using a quarter of a dye disc. Pour the wax over the thermometer into the mould.

3. When the wax has set, carefully remove some of the sand from the bucket and then lift out the sand candle. Some of the wax will have seeped into the sand, forming a decorative container for the candle and leaving quite a deep well in the centre of the wax block.

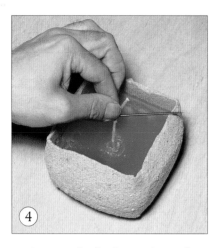

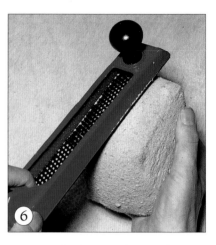

4. Pierce a hole down through the middle of the wax using a wicking needle. Insert a waxed wick and support it in position with the wicking needle.

5. Top up the well with wax then allow it to cool. Remove the wicking needle.

6. Smooth the roughness from the outer surfaces of the sand container with a coarse file. You could now leave the candle as it is, or you could decorate it as shown in steps 7 and 8.

Carving on sand candles

When carving a design on sand candles, it is easier to work with a warmed surface. To do this, carefully heat the area you are going to work on with a hairdryer.

7. To decorate your candle, mark out a design on the sides of the sand container using an old pair of dividers.

8. Use a metal modelling tool to scrape away the sand around the design and reveal the outer layer of the candle.

Stencilled candles

Use a repeat pattern to create delicate effects. Stencils are available from most craft suppliers and they can be used to create borders or motifs.

Before you begin, check that the stencil you have chosen will cover the surface of the candle, then fix the stencil in place with tape. Follow the manufacturer's instructions and lightly coat the surface with paint. Do not worry about a smooth finish – textured effects can be attractive, especially in candlelight.

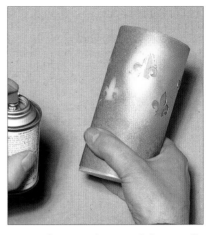

Wrap the stencil around the candle and secure with tape. Hold the can of spray paint a short distance away and apply it in short bursts. Allow the paint to dry before carefully removing the stencil.

Gold spray paint is here used on white candles to create a special finish.

Surface texture

Interesting and decorative textures can be moulded into the surface of a candle if you use corrugated paper to line the inside of a mould with. You will need a silicon release agent, which is available as an aerosol or as a liquid. Cut the paper to fit neatly inside the mould. Try to avoid overlapping edges, as these will be visible on the finished candle. Remove the paper from the mould and apply the silicon release agent to both sides. Replace the paper in the mould, insert a wick and then make the candle as shown on pages 17–19. When cool, the candle will slide easily from the mould, and the paper can be peeled away to reveal the textured wax surface.

These candles are made using corrugated paper to line the mould and so give texture. The candles use the same technique as shown on page 17–19.

Appliquéd candles

These candles are ideal for special occasions. Work on a surface coated with greaseproof paper and cut out small motifs from bought wax sheets with pastry cutters. Apply the motifs to the candle surface with wax glue. If the motifs cool too quickly and are no longer malleable, warm them gently with a hairdryer. Press them on to the curved surface of the candle, and secure them with melted wax glue.

You can decorate your candles by sticking on cut-out wax motifs using wax glue.

Painting with wax

Melted coloured wax is the best medium for painting on wax. It is important to colour the wax with candle pigment, as dyes tend to migrate. Keep the wax warm while you paint – an egg poacher makes an ideal palette. Use an ordinary artist's brush and work with smooth strokes. The wax cools quickly, so re-dip the brush frequently, leaving the brush in the warm wax for at least twenty seconds, so that any wax that has solidified on the brush is completely melted.

Candles can be decorated by brushing on coloured wax.

Transfers

Designs can be added to the candle surface using water transfers. Soak the transfers in water for thirty seconds, then remove one and slip the design on to the candle. It should come away from its paper base easily.

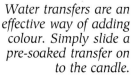

Water transfers are an effective way of adding colour. Simply slide a pre-soaked transfer on to the candle.

45

Faults

Listed here are some of the common problems likely to be encountered when making dipped and moulded candles, the probable reasons for them and what best to do about them.

Dipping

FAULT	CAUSE	WHAT TO DO
Lumpy surface on candle	First dip too fast. Wax too cold while dipping.	While candle is still warm roll it on a smooth surface.
Candle spits whilst burning	Water in candle.	Pour off molten wax and relight candle. If this is not successful, then remelt it.
White marks in layers of dip candles	Wax too cold whilst dipping.	An eight-second dip in wax at 93°C (200°F) may be successful.
Candle cracks whilst rolling	Uneven temperature throughout candle, i.e. the centre may be harder than the surface of the candle.	Re-dip candle until pliable.
Damaged or old candle	Age, dirt, fading, etc.	Rub over surface with nylon stocking and white spirit. Decorate to cover flaws.

Casting in moulds

FAULT	CAUSE	WHAT TO DO
Air bubbles on surface	Poured too fast. Placed in water bath too soon. Dust in mould. Mould not tapped to remove air.	Pour slowly. Wait for one minute before placing in water bath. Clean mould. Tap mould one minute after pouring.
Cracks throughout candle	Candle allowed to become too cold before topping up.	Use water bath at room temperate.

FAULT	CAUSE	WHAT TO DO
Seepage between candle and mould	Wax allowed to set and contract away from the side of the mould, allowing some of the topping-up wax to seep down the side.	Cut off the unwanted marks.
Loss of definition with a layered candle	Previously poured wax not set sufficiently to support the next layer. The surface should be rubbery.	Remelt. Remember that the resulting wax will be a combination of colours, usually brown.
Layers not joining	Wax poured too late or at too low a temperate.	Remelt.
Misshapen candle; sides caved in	Surface around wick not broken and probed soon enough. Air in centre of candle.	Keep surface constantly broken until candle is almost set.
Soap-like appearance	Too much stearin added.	Check proportion of wax mixture.
Candle will not come out of a rigid mould	Not enough stearin added. Candle topped up above the original level, causing seepage between candle and mould. Cooling too slow, resulting in insufficient contraction.	Place in hot water and melt candle out of mould. Alternatively, place in refrigerator for twenty minutes.
Candle will not come out of flexible mould	Candle left to get too cold before removal	Place in hot water and melt the candle out of the mould.
Ring of discolouration around top of candle	Dirty wax.	Take more care. Keep moulds and utensils clean.
Scaly marks on surface	Wax poured too cold for prevailing room temperature.	Use a water bath. Pour at a higher temperature.
Mould leaking from base	Careless wicking-up. Damaged mould.	Seal with mould seal. Place candle in water bath immediately.
Small bubbly line encircling candle	Mark of water-level from water bath. Water added after candle placed in bath.	Rub with nylon stocking. Fill water bath almost to top of mould level before putting mould in.

Index